ROCK-OLOGY
The Hard Facts
About Rocks

How Do Water and Wind Change Rock?

A Look at Sedimentary Rock

by Ellen Lawrence

Consultants:

Shawn W. Wallace
Department of Earth and Planetary Sciences
American Museum of Natural History, New York, New York

Kimberly Brenneman, PhD
National Institute for Early Education Research, Rutgers University
New Brunswick, New Jersey

BEARPORT
PUBLISHING

New York, New York

Credits

Cover: © Francesco R. Lacomino/Shutterstock; 2–3, © Johnny Adolphson/Shutterstock; 4–5, © Francesco R. Lacomino/Shutterstock; 6, © Marco Poplasen/Shutterstock; 7L, © Leene/Shutterstock; 7C, © Ian Woolcock/Shutterstock; 7R, © Tupungato/Shutterstock; 8, © My Life Graphic/Shutterstock and © Siim Sepp/Wikipedia Creative Commons; 9, © Konstantnin/Shutterstock; 10–11, © Shutterstock; 12, © Shutterstock; 13, © SIHASAKPRACHUM/Shutterstock; 14, © Florian Wirsing/istockphoto; 15, © Marisa Estivill/Shutterstock; 16, © urosr/Shutterstock; 17, © Siim Sepp/Shutterstock; 18, © Public Domain; 19, © Derek Croucher/Alamy; 20, © Danie Nel/Shutterstock; 21, © michal812/Shutterstock, © kavring/Shutterstock, © Dr. Ajay Kumar Singh/Shutterstock, © Siim Sepp/Shutterstock, © vvoe/Shutterstock, © Elena Burn/Shutterstock, © jirawat/Shutterstock, and © Tyler Boyes/Shutterstock; 22, © xpixel/Shutterstock, © bogdan ionescu/Shutterstock, © Mariyana M/Shutterstock, and © Mauro Rodrigues/Shutterstock; 23TL, © Malgorzata Litkowska/Shutterstock; 23TC, © Ron Ellis/Shutterstock; 23TR, © Les Palenik/Shutterstock; 23BL, © Nastya22/Shutterstock; 23BC, © Marko Poplasen/Shutterstock; 23BR, © suronin/Shutterstock.

Publisher: Kenn Goin
Editorial Director: Adam Siegel
Creative Director: Spencer Brinker
Project Editor: Natalie Lunis
Photo Researcher: Ruby Tuesday Books Ltd

Library of Congress Cataloging-in-Publication Data

Lawrence, Ellen, 1967– author.
 How do water and wind change rock? : a look at sedimentary rock / by Ellen Lawrence.
     pages cm. — (Rock-ology)
 Audience: Ages 7–12
 Includes bibliographical references and index.
 ISBN 978-1-62724-299-8 (library binding) — ISBN 1-62724-299-6 (library binding)
 1. Sedimentary rocks—Juvenile literature. 2. Petrology—Juvenile literature. 3. Weathering—Juvenile literature. I. Title.
 QE471.L36 2015
 552.5—dc23
                          2014014032

For more information, write to Bearport Publishing Company, Inc., 45 West 21st Street, Suite 3B, New York, New York 10010. Printed in the United States of America.

10 9 8 7 6 5 4 3 2 1

Contents

A Wave in the Desert

In a desert in Arizona, there is a rock **formation** called The Wave.

Its slopes curve up and down.

They have a pattern made up of reddish-brown and white stripes.

How did this rocky place form?

The Wave is made of rock that is more than 150 million years old. It formed during the time when dinosaurs lived on Earth.

The Wave

Why do you think this rock formation is called The Wave?

What Is The Wave Made Of?

The Wave is made of sandstone.

Sandstone is a kind of **sedimentary** rock.

All sedimentary rock forms from tiny pieces of rock called **sediment**.

Where does the sediment come from?

sediment

Look at this picture of sediment. What words would you use to describe it?

6

Sandstone is a kind of sedimentary rock.

Granite is a kind of igneous rock.

Gneiss (NICE) is a kind of metamorphic rock.

Scientists sort Earth's rocks into three main groups. They are called sedimentary, **igneous**, and **metamorphic** rock. Each type of rock forms in a different way.

Making Sediment

Sometimes sediment forms when it rains.

As rainwater washes over large rocks, it wears them away.

Tiny pieces of rock break off from the larger rocks.

These tiny rocky pieces will go on to form sedimentary rock.

How does this happen?

Sand is a type of sediment. If you look at it through a magnifying glass, you can see that each grain is made of rock.

sediment

Sediment on the Move

Sometimes rainwater washes sediment into a lake.

Other times, sediment may be washed into a river.

Then the river carries the sediment into a lake.

Here, the sediment settles on the bottom.

Over thousands of years, more sediment is washed into the lake.

Layer upon layer of sediment builds up on the lake's bottom.

Not all pieces of sediment start out small. Sometimes big chunks are washed into rivers. As the rushing river water carries them along, however, these big pieces crash into each other. Then they break into smaller and smaller pieces.

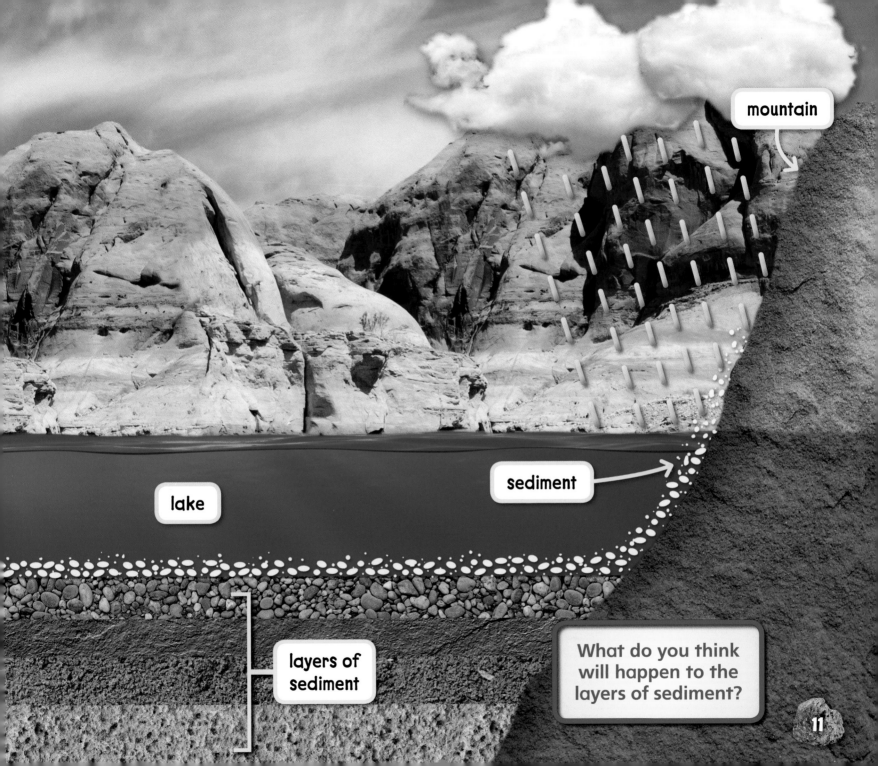

mountain

sediment

lake

layers of sediment

What do you think will happen to the layers of sediment?

Turning into Rock

The layers of sediment at the bottom of the lake press together.

Over millions of years, they join to become new sedimentary rock.

Sedimentary rock often has layers that are different colors.

That's because each layer of sediment may have come from a different kind of rock.

Like all rock, sediment is made up of substances called **minerals**. Some minerals help to cement the pieces of sediment together—just like the cement that joins bricks together in a brick wall.

sediment washed into the lake

layers of sediment

layers of sediment that have become rock

These sandstone rocks in China formed millions of years ago.

Making Rock with Wind

Sedimentary rock can form in another way, too.

Sometimes the wind blows and picks up loose pieces of sand or dirt.

When flying sand or dirt rubs against large rocks, it causes tiny pieces to break off.

This sediment settles in layers on the ground.

Over millions of years, more and more layers build up.

The layers of sediment join together to make new sedimentary rock.

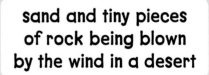

sand and tiny pieces
of rock being blown
by the wind in a desert

The sandstone rock of The Wave was formed from sediment made by the wind. It's possible to see the different colors of the sediment in the rock's layers.

Shaping The Wave

The Wave didn't always look like it does today.

When the sandstone rock first formed, it did not have smooth, curved slopes.

So what made the rock's rippling, wave-like curves?

It took millions of years, but dusty winds carved The Wave's incredible shape.

As they swirled and swirled over the rock, tiny pieces broke off and were carried away.

The Wave

What did The Wave look like before the wind created its unusual shape? It was probably a rough sandstone formation like the one in this picture.

The Old Man of Hoy

The Wave isn't the only amazing rock formation made from sedimentary rock.

The Old Man of Hoy on the Scottish island of Hoy is another one.

This rocky tower was once joined to the sandstone cliff behind it.

Over hundreds of years, however, ocean waves crashed into the cliff, wearing away the rock.

During this time, large chunks of the cliff fell away, leaving the tower standing alone.

This painting shows how the Old Man of Hoy looked 100 years ago.

The Old Man of Hoy is as tall as a 40-story building. The tower got its name because it used to look like a person standing on two legs.

Old Man of Hoy

sandstone cliff

layers of sedimentary rock

19

Rock Hunting

Many people like to collect and study rocks as a hobby.

They are known as rockhounds.

Rockhounds know that there are many kinds of sedimentary rocks.

All of these rocks formed from sediment, but they look very different.

That's what makes rock collecting so much fun!

Rockhounds find rocks in deserts, on mountains and rocky hillsides, and at the beach. It's even possible to find rocks in backyards and parks.

Sedimentary Rocks Chart

Sandstone is one kind of sedimentary rock. There are many other kinds as well. All of these solid chunks of rock were once many tiny grains of sediment.

Sandstone (SAND-*stohn*)	**Breccia** (BREH-chee-uh)	**Limestone** (LIME-*stohn*)
Flint (FLINT)	**Conglomerate** (kuhn-GLOM-ur-it)	**Dolomite** (DOH-luh-*mite*)
Banded ironstone (BAND-id EYE-urn-*stohn*)	**Shale** (SHAYL)	**Chert** (CHURT)

Science Lab

Make Sedimentary Rock in a Jar

Using real sediment, such as sand and pebbles, you can make a model that shows how sedimentary rock forms.

You will need:
- Spoon
- Sand
- Empty glass jar with lid
- Gravel or pebbles

1. Spoon some sand into the jar. Press it down with the spoon.

2. Add a layer of pebbles. Then add a third layer of sediment that's different from the one below.

3. Keep adding layers, pressing down on each one with the spoon.

4. When your jar is full, screw on the lid tightly.

Share your model with your family, friends, or teacher. Explain how the layers of sediment in your jar are similar to the layers that form at the bottom of a lake and become rock.

Science Words

formation (for-MAY-shuhn) a group of rocks or a large rock that stands out in an interesting way or has an unusual shape

igneous (IG-nee-uhss) one of the three main types of rock; basalt, gabbro, and granite are kinds of igneous rock

metamorphic (*met-uh-MOR-fik*) one of the three main types of rock; marble, slate, and gneiss are kinds of metamorphic rock

minerals (MIN-ur-uhlz) the solid substances found in nature that make up rocks

sediment (SED-uh-muhnt) tiny pieces of rock that have broken away from a larger rock; pebbles and grains of sand are both types of sediment

sedimentary (*sed-uh-MEN-tuh-ree*) one of the three main types of rock; sandstone, limestone, and shale are kinds of sedimentary rock

Index

Read More

Faulkner, Rebecca. *Sedimentary Rock (Geology Rocks!).* Chicago, IL: Raintree (2007).

Rosinsky, Maria. *Rocks: Hard, Soft, Smooth, and Rough.* Minneapolis, MN: Picture Window Books (2003).

Owen, Ruth. *Science and Craft Projects with Rocks and Soil (Get Crafty Outdoors).* New York: PowerKids Press (2013).

Learn More Online

To learn more about sedimentary rock, visit www.bearportpublishing.com/Rock-ology

About the Author

Ellen Lawrence lives in the United Kingdom. Her favorite books to write are those about nature and animals. In fact, the first book Ellen bought for herself, when she was six years old, was the story of a gorilla named Patty Cake that was born in New York's Central Park Zoo.